Eric Mackay

A Song of the Sea

My Lady of Dreams - And Other Poems

Eric Mackay

A Song of the Sea
My Lady of Dreams - And Other Poems

ISBN/EAN: 9783337007218

Printed in Europe, USA, Canada, Australia, Japan

Cover: Foto ©Thomas Meinert / pixelio.de

More available books at **www.hansebooks.com**

A SONG OF THE SEA
MY LADY OF DREAMS

AND OTHER POEMS

BY

ERIC MACKAY

AUTHOR OF "LOVE LETTERS OF A VIOLINIST"

METHUEN & CO.
36 ESSEX STREET, LONDON
1895

CONTENTS

	PAGE
A Song of the Sea : Ode for Imperial Federation	7
My Lady of Dreams	18
Shelley's Monument at Via Reggio	26
The Prince's Return from Russia	31
The Lark's Song in April	35
Lines to a Dead Bard	42
Man the Fleet!	49
The Falls of Foyers	53
Sea Voices	57
The Quelétzû	62
The Dead Tsar	67
A Love Song	74
The Death Day of Tennyson	76
Thorns	82
Moushka	87

CONTENTS

ODES—

	PAGE
The Royal Marriage Ode	97
A Choral Ode to Liberty	120
Hymn to the Rising Sun	132
The White Rose of the Crown	138
Ode to an Ideal Poet	146
The Song of the Flag	153

A SONG OF THE SEA

AN ODE FOR IMPERIAL FEDERATION

I

FREE as the wind that leaps from out the North,
When storms are hurrying forth,
Up-springs the voice of England, trumpet-clear,
Which all the world shall hear,
As one may hear God's thunder over-head,—
A voice that echoes through the sunset red,
And through the fiery portals of the morn
Where, day by day, the golden hours are born,—
A voice to urge the strengthening of the bands

That bind our Empire Lands
With such a love as none shall put to scorn!

II

They little know our England who deny
The claim we have, from zone to furthest zone,
To belt the beauteous earth,
And treat the clamorous ocean as our own
In all the measuring of its monstrous girth.
The tempest calls to us, and we reply;
And not, as cowards do, in under-tone!
The sun that sets for others sets no more
On Britain's world-wide shore
Which all the tides of all the seas have known.

III

Our ways are on the waters wan and wild,
When cloud on cloud, up-piled,

Reveal the fume and frenzy of the blast
That shrills and hurries past,
As if to wreck a ship unseen of Heaven,
Ere yet the dreadful levin
Rips up the dark with fingers as of fire;
And there we sate our strength and our desire
In thuds of storm and buffetings of fate;
And there we conquer in the glad sun's ken,
And there we lie unceasingly in wait
For wondrous morrows unforeseen of men.

IV

The ocean, the great ocean, loves us much,
And all those ships of ours that we have manned;
Aye, and it revels in the tremulous touch
Of our sweet margin-sand;
And on its bosom wears in shine and shower,
As women wear a flower,

Each new-annexed dominion of the Crown,
To be the trophy of our widening power,—
An isle of fair renown
Where Britons build a bulwark or a town,—
Or some out-lying length of heathen soil
Where swart, ungodly men are taught to pray,
And do the deeds of prowess and of toil.
For so the sponsors of our ocean-might
Have re-affirmed the reasons of the right
Of our triumphant rule in war and peace;
And none shall daunt us, none shall say us
    nay,
Or bid the pageant of our glories cease.

V

We have no lust of strife:
We seek no vile dissension for base ends;
Freedom and fame and England are old
    friends!

We have a sword for valour,—not a knife
For Murder's work in history; and we know
What truths we taught the foe
At well-fought Trafalgàr!
Who doubts us when our armies are a-field,
With our good flag revealed,
And every fold thereof a triumph-sign
To tell of martial feats achieved afar,
Beyond earth's central line?
But ours a better, ours a holier creed,
Than wounds and waste and wantonness of
    deed
That turn to glory in the after-shine.
For we have shown that Victory is not dumb
When Peace and Pity plead for Brotherhood;
And evermore, unshent, we have withstood
The claims and clamours of down-treading
    war.
Yet if our foes desire it, let them come,

Whate'er their numbers be !
They know the road to England, mile by
    mile,
And they shall learn, full soon, that strength
    nor guile
Will much avail them in an English sea ;
We will not hurl them backward to the
    waves,—
We'll give them graves !

VI

'Tis much to be so honoured in the main,
And feel no further stain
Than one's own blood out-poured in lieu of
    wine.
'Tis much to die in England, and for this
To win the sabre-kiss
Of some true man who deems his cause divine,
And loves his country well.

A foe may calmly dwell
In our sweet soil with daisies for his quilt,—
Their snows to hide his guilt,
And earth's good warmth about him where
  he lies
Beyond the burden of all battle-cries,
And made half-English by his resting-place :—
God give him grace !

VII

For when the century's tale is aptly told,
This much will come to light ;
We were the first in fight
And first in commerce all the wide world
  through.
Witness the deeds we do !
The quick resolves that prove our better
  worth,
When foes wax over-bold ;

And all the trystes that evermore we keep
With those our fierce adherents on the deep:—
The north-wind and the east, the fearful twain
Who strip the woods in winter, and make mirth
On many a ravished plain,—
The Boreal brothers who are quick to bear
Earth's message through the air,
And mix their meanings with the billows' roar
In some terrific tune,
Well known on every surf-tormented shore,—
As if the judgment-day were come too soon,
And Hell were loosened on the ocean-tracks,
And all the waves had riders on their backs!

VIII

We love the sea,—the loud, the leaping sea,—
The rush and roar of waters,—the thick foam,—
The sea-bird's sudden cry,—

The gale that bends the lithe and towering masts
Of good ships bounding home,
That spread to the great sky
Exultant flags unmatched in their degree!
And 'tis a joy that lasts,
A joy that thrills the Briton to the soul
Who knows the nearest goal
To all he asks of fortune and of fame,
From dusk to dawn and dawn to sunset-flame.
He knows that he is free,
With all the freedom of the waves and winds
That have the storm in fee;
And evermore he seeks what there he finds:—
A hope, a joy, a certainty of strength,
Beyond the Empire's length,
And, year by year, he pleads for Federation
With such acclaim as fits a jubilation!

IX

We were the Ocean's children from the first;
We toyed with fate, we dallied with the shocks
Of wrack and ravin; and, unscathed thereby,
We dared calamity to do its worst.
We taught our foes to die!
We set our mark on sea-confronting rocks,
To urge our right of way; and,—stroke by stroke,—
We scoured the waters clean of pirate-folk;
And, fired with faith in all that we had vowed,
We brought the scourge of slavery to an end.
We made the wind our comrade and our friend,
And called to it aloud,—
And where it led, we followed and were proud,—
The wind that roars its octave to the thunder,
When danger has the darkness in its grip :—

The wind that gives the key-note to the storm,
And moulds the monstrous form
Of many a weltering wave with hungering lip,
When,—with a word of warning,—or of wonder,—
The sea's great voice intones
Its monody of madness and of moans.

X

And this our glory still :—to bear the palm
In all true enterprise,
And everywhere, in tempest and in calm,
To front the future with unfearing eyes,
And sway the seas where our advancement lies,
With Freedom's flag uplifted, and unfurled ;
And this our rallying-cry, whate'er befall,
Good-will to men, and peace throughout the world,
But England,—England,—England over all !

MY LADY OF DREAMS

I

HAVE you met in the glade,
When the breezes are laid,
The delight of my soul with her passionate
    eyes,
That are large with the lures
Of a love that endures,—
As an angel's, enthroned in the scintillant skies,
Who has looked on the face
Of the Giver of Grace?

II

Have you seen her at night,
When the moon's at the height

Of its glory and glamour approved of the
    stars,—
Have you seen her untwist,
Like a maiden of mist,
Or a newly-descended effulgence of Mars,
All her tresses divine
That are Summer's,—and mine?

III

She's a sylph of the air
With her mantle of hair
That's alit with the rays of the refluent sun;
And the hills and the plains
Of her magic domains
Are the haunts of the fairies when daylight is
    done,
And the birthplace of words
That are wingèd as birds!

IV

It is she,—it is she,
Who has waited for me
In the woods and the wilds of the valleys of
    sleep;
It is she who has brought,
By the pulsings of thought,
All the songs that I love, all the records I
    keep,—
All the hopes and the fears
That are hallowed by tears.

V

And I know in my heart,
When I tremble and start
At the sob of the wind, at the sigh of the
    breeze,
That the lady I sing
Is the boast of the spring,

And the pride of the meadows out there by
 the trees,
And the bearer of news
From the grass and the dews.

VI

I shall revel ere long,
In a joy that is strong
With the strength of a sorrow unseated at last;
For the whisper, meseems,
Of my Lady of Dreams
Is a dearer reward than a trumpeter's blast,
That announces a name
In the tourneys of Fame.

VII

She is known unto men,
On the moor, in the glen,

As a melody's known that is true to the core;
She's acclaimed in the bowers
As the queen of the flowers;
And there's nothing that lives on the sea or
    the shore
That is hid from her gaze
In the nights and the days.

VIII

She is one of the choir
Of the daughters of fire,
And the touch of her hand is a token of truth;
And her presence is sweet,
From the face to the feet,
With the fervour of love and the joyance of
    youth,
And the sense of a trust
That out-liveth the dust.

IX

When I meet her alone,
And the day's overthrown,
And the gloaming comes on, like the silence itself,
I shall feel it is true,
As she glides into view,
That her sire was a vision,—her mother an elf
Whom the poets have seen
In the gardens terrene.

X

In the whispered lament
Of a breeze that is spent,
In the murmur thereof I shall know she is nigh;
In the hush of the snows,
In the blush of the rose,

In the droop of the lily that's weighed with
　　a sigh,
I shall trace her appeal
In the rapture I feel.

XI

I shall guess what is said
Of the quick and the dead ;
I shall know what is best to enshrine or
　　destroy ;
And the lore of the lute,
And the taste of the fruit
That the seasons have touched with the
　　tremors of joy,
Will be mine to possess,
In her sainted caress.

XII

For my Lady is wise
With a wisdom that flies

From the sun to the star, from the star to the
 flower;
And she floats to my arms,
In her mystical charms,
With the wealth of the wonder of song for a
 dower,—
Yet all that she saith
Is revealed in a breath!

SHELLEY'S MONUMENT AT VIA REGGIO

I

THE sea that claimed our Shelley holds him not,
  And Via Reggio pleads for him in vain;
  The barque that foundered on a foreign main
Is curst of all good men, and nigh forgot.
But he who sailed therein has made his lot
  The Muse's glory, and his country's gain.

II.

We cannot spare our poet for the south,
  Or for the sea that slew him long ago;

His youth was reared in England, as we know,
And Freedom sated all his singing-drouth,
And called him hers, and kissed him on the mouth,
And made him wise with all the winds that blow.

III

If Time require a monument for thee,
   We'll have a nobler one than alien hands
   Can build thee, Shelley! on Italian sands;
And if thy face must front a foaming sea,
We have our share of ocean that is free,
   And here we'll shrine thee as thy fame demands.

IV

Not Rome thy resting-place from year to year,
   Not that Italia where thy days were spent,

To our remorse, and thine own detriment.
Thou hast thy home with us in England here,
And not out there, where Fortune was austere,
 And burnt the form that malice never bent.

V

'Twas Byron wept for thee, when from the pyre
 Trelawny tore the heart that beat in tune
 With all the hearts of men in mystic rune.
For hellish flames could not consume the lyre
That throbbed with joy for every soul's desire,
 And filled the earth with songs from June to June.

VI

Yes, Byron wept; and we,—unfit to weep
 Unless for mere self-pity,—lo! we turn

With lips apart, and eyes that sea-ward
   yearn,
To greet yon Tuscans while their tryste they
   keep
With our dead singer, wakened out of sleep
   To teach the creeds the world is slow to
   learn.

VII

God's truth! Is't well? Whose words were
   those he flung
   From his proud lips, accordant with the roll
   Of star with star, and soul with human
   soul?
Whose words? Our own,—our England's
   golden tongue,
Long centuries old, and yet divinely young
   As this day's dawn that shines from pole
   to pole!

VIII

'Tis we,—not they,—who call thee from the past,
  'Tis we invoke, from realms where none are drowned,
  Thy presence, Shelley! wronged on English ground,
But righted now,—as all men are at last,—
And safe beyond opprobrium's bitter blast ;
  For thou art crowned as Shakespeare's self is crowned !

THE PRINCE'S RETURN FROM RUSSIA

DECEMBER 6, 1894

I

WHAT news to-day?
What soundings of the sea?
What message of the morning to the Land
That's circled round about with frontier-sand?
What note of war in what unwonted key
To bid the world be armed for such affray
As dyes with valiant blood the salt sea-foam?
Has some great voice imperial in the North
Vouchsafed a word supreme,
With Progress as the outcome of its theme?

Or what's the deed that calls our plaudits
 forth?—
Our English Prince comes home!

II

He brings us greetings from an alien shore
That's loud with ocean's unsubmissive roar,
And leapings of wild waves,
O'er which the storm-wind raves.
He tells us not of battles lost or won,
Or sailors' wandering graves,
Or deeds of danger, darkly to be done
Beneath an outraged, unapproving sun.
He brings us friendly vows from foreign lips,
And rumours of concessions due to us
For our dear Land's renown!
And who shall say that, home-returning thus,
He comes not back more welcome to us all
Than if he brought us news of routed ships,

And foemen trampled down,
In some beleaguered town,
To sate a tyrant's unremitting thrall?

III

All praise to him who sheathes his sword in trust
Of what the years may teach without a crime!
'Tis much to wound a foe;
'Tis more to save him and to win a friend,
This side the surging of the seas of Time,
Whose wherewithal shall no man truly know
Till power and pomp and pride are laid in dust;
For he alone is great who dares be just!
He conquers well who conquers with a word;
And ere the spring comes round
A Russian name for Freedom may be found!
Promise of dawn is only day deferred,

And Truth and Sunrise are of kindred fire
To wake the wonders of the world's desire,
And unto him the loveliest wreath belongs
Who bids dissensions cease,
And vaunts no battle-star,—
For he is rich indeed who's poor in wrongs :—
He is a victor who out-victors war
And plants his banner on the heights of Peace!

THE LARK'S SONG IN APRIL

I

O ECHOING Voice that o'er the woodlands wide,
Dost warble, at spring-tide,
Of hope and love that hold the world in sway,
What news dost bring to-day
Of those fair fields of dawn where light is sanctified?

II

From out the roseate cloud, athwart the blue,
I hear thee sound anew
That song of thine, a-shimmering down the sky;

And daisies, touched thereby,
Look up to thee in tears which men mistake
    for dew.

III

There is no bird a-field, or in the air,
Which can with thee compare
When to thy lord, the sun, thou dost impart
In faithfulness of heart,
The thanks of mead and mere for all the joys
    they share.

IV

Thou art indeed the spokesman of the flowers,
Which have no singing-powers,
And with their perfume all thy blood's a-stir;
And thou dost mix with myrrh
The maddening strains that fall from those
    thy skyward bowers.

V

There's no such trill as thine, or east or west,
And no such wild unrest;
And he were chief of bards who'd learn from thee,
That hast the master-key,
The song of earth's goodwill that's wafted from a nest.

VI

I see thee clip the air, and rush and reel,
As if excess of zeal
Had giddied thee in thy chromatic joys;
And overhead dost poise
With outstretched wings of love that bless while they appeal.

VII

'Tis true that summer's near us as thou say'st,
With all its fruits to taste,
And lilies, too, and clambering eglantine,
And roses red as wine,
And flowers that maidens wear, with love-knots interlaced.

VIII

'Tis true that love's the theme of all the notes
That come from sylvan throats,
And that thy friends, the linnet and the thrush,
Have met, at evening-blush,
To hail thee bard of morn by all their dulcet votes.

IX

What!—back within the cloud?—or where art thou,
That all quiescent now

Dost seem to pause awhile in thine emprize?
Hast bounded through the skies?
Or dost but hide thee there, to con some
    golden vow?

X

Thy ways are not as ours, thou joyous bird!
Thou quick incarnate Word!
And all in vain I watch thee in thy flight;
Nor can I guess aright
What thoughts of sweet content within thy
    heart are stirred.

XI

So far away thy wings have wafted thee
O'er yon cerulean sea,
That much I fear to lose thee, little one,

Ere yet thy song be done,—
And this were gain to Heaven, but loss to mine and me.

XII

Ah,—thou'rt in sight once more, thou heart's desire!
Thou feathery floating fire!
And round and round dost spin and wilt not cease;
For flight to thee is peace,
And song's a kind of rage that goads thee to aspire.

XIII

Thou hast within thy throat a peal of bells,
Dear dainty fare-thee-wells,
And like a flame dost leap from cloud to cloud:—

Is't this that makes thee proud?
Or is't that nest of thine deep-hidden in the
dells?

XIV

Whate'er thy meaning be, or vaunt or prayer,
I know thy home is there;
And when I hear thee trill, as now thou dost,
I take the world on trust,
And with the world thyself, thou foeman of
despair!

LINES TO A DEAD BARD

I

LIVING, but dead,—as some neglected weed
That's flung aside, forgotten by the spring,—
Who cares of thee to sing
That, with the fœtor of polluted breath,
And out-come of foul seed,
Hast shamed the sweetness of our English bowers?
Poets who love the flowers
Love not thy presence there, in life or death;
And birds in haste depart,
And all good things avoid thee like a curse!
For Nature loathes thee; and 'tis past the skill
Of drugs to cure thee of thy venom'd ill,

And past the power of prosody or verse
To say how vile thou art!

II

Poet no more!—thy place is with the dead;
The quick reject thee as a thing unclean,—
A scare-crow of the Muses,—a swoll'n head
Mouthing it knows not what, in words ob-
    scene!
Poets have heart and feeling,—thou hast none;
But, in their stead, convulsion and a shriek
That's meant for fervour, when thine accents
    run
From that dazed brain of thine that's grown
    so weak.
Go, tell the world that Byron was no bard,
And thou a Shelley—in thine own regard!
Jabber of fame, and squeak of what will
    come

When thy shrill voice in these confines is
    dumb,—
And bid all men be brothers,—in despair!
Tell them that truth's a lie, and faith a snare,
And hope a word for children,—or for fools:
Bid them denounce the Christ as thou hast
    done,
And ban religion from the public schools,
With only pedant-rules
To serve as guide in lands beyond the sun.
Aye!—tell them God's a myth, and Heaven
    a dream,—
But thou thyself a something that exists
With peepy eyes and palsy-stricken wrists
To mark the measure of thy rhythmic
    scream!
Tell them all this and more,—for more's
    behind
Which by-and-by the world will call to mind,—

And, when 'tis uttered, say that "one
 unknown"
Has done thee justice on thy puny throne!

III

Thou,—king of bards? *Thou*,—wielder of a
 pen
That sways the nations? May God help us
 then!
If song were gin, a man might turn to thee
To test its strength, and help thee find the
 key
That opes that cupboard where thy Demon
 dwells,—
The fiend of drink which goads while it repels,
And gives thee semblance of poetic fire
Which is not Heaven's indeed, but lowest
 Hell's,
And fills thy veins with lustful base desire

And makes us blush to own that, for a
  time,
We heeded thee and thy poor gift of rhyme.

IV

Drink, bard of bottles! Bard of kisses caught
From some mean drab of verse whose name
  is naught!
Aye, 'drink thy fill,—and, drinking, make it
  plain
That thy Silenus-strain
Is meant for mischief now as heretofore!
Who deemed his voice a lion's by its roar?—
Though few could hear it,—fifty times belied
And laughed at, too, through all the country-
  side,—
And who believed, a-tip-toe at the news,
That he alone was "master" of the Muse?

V

Fie, man, for shame! We have our Byron yet,
And Keats, and Shelley, and the golden throng
Of those sweet singers who to fame belong,
And whom the world is powerless to forget.
If thou could'st sing as these it would be well;
If thou could'st soar as high, and look on things
As they can look, with sunlight on their wings,—
Nor I nor those who spurn thee would rebel
Against thy dictum:—But thy reign is o'er,—
If reign it was,—and half thy lyric store
Is proved ill-gotten; part of ancient date
And part usurped, or plagiarised of late
From better books than thou can'st write withal!

O shamed and shameless, whom the Furies call,
But not the Muses!—O thou unbesought
Of cleanly folk and scholars pure of thought!
Vent, if thou wilt, thy rancour and thy rage
Because neglect has claimed thee for its own,
But cease to vex the age
With all that yelping,— and that lack of tone,—
Which prove thee but a false pretender still.
Gnaw thy remorse as dogs may gnaw a bone,
But haunt no more Apollo's sacred hill;
The sun-god knows thee for a vagrant there,
And spurns thee forth as poison to the air!

MAN THE FLEET

I

Hark! a voice that from afar
Calls from fort and harbour-bar,
  Man the Fleet!
Loud and long and clear it rings,
As when some one boldly sings,
Fired with faith in noble things,—
  Man the Fleet!

II

Deaf are those who cannot hear
England's cry from year to year,
  Man the Fleet!
Blind are they who will not see

Why the Fates have kept us free—
Why we're strong as men should be.
> Man the Fleet!

III

This the warning—this the shout—
Born of truths we cannot doubt,
> Man the Fleet!

Keep the country's coast secure,
Launch the word that's loud and sure;
Keep the standard proud and pure!
> Man the Fleet!

IV

When our Nelson faced the foam
All his ships were glory's home.
> Man the Fleet!

England hears his spirit call
O'er the wide and watery wall;

"Each for each, and God for all!"
      Man the Fleet!

V

Nelson's name is one with fame,
Sweet as song, and fair as flame.
      Man the Fleet!
When he lived he waved on high
England's flag to sea and sky;
Now—though dead—he cannot die!
      Man the Fleet!

VI

His the frown that scared the foe,
His the sword that laid them low,
      Man the Fleet!
His the glance that in the past
Saw, when skies were overcast,
England's star supreme at last!
      Man the Fleet!

VII

Red, and white, and blue as dawn
Gleams the flag we doat upon.
> Man the Fleet!

And the sun, that's daily crowned
King of all the ocean round,
Loves our good ships where they bound;
> Man the Fleet!

VIII

None shall daunt us, east or west;
North or south shall none molest!
> Man the Fleet!

Give the lie to those who fear!
Voice the cry and make it clear—
Make it plain—that all may hear;
> Man the Fleet!

THE FALLS OF FOYERS

A Protest against their Threatened
Destruction

I

Out of the North a rumour, big with shame,
Has reached us here in England, undenied
By Scotia's voice of pride,
Which never yet has failed us in the field,—
A rumour fraught with outrage, ill-concealed,
That burns, as with a flame,
The sense we have of justice and of truth.
For soon a hand audacious and uncouth
Will mar the might of Nature in the glen
That's dear as fame itself to all true men,—

An upland-place of beauty,—a delight,
A power, a pomp, a wonder,—a desire
That knows the Morning's fire,
And Sunset's glow and glamour on the height.

II

And whose the fiat, whose the fell command
That makes a mock of history and of song,
And, all the summer, all the winter long,
Would silence Foyers? and rob the lovely land
Of God's decree of glory? Curst be they
Who dare do this and live!
The world has much to take, and much to give,
And much to cast away;
But not the Falls of Foyers, the great Falls,
With their time-honoured sway,

And their triumphant calls
To cloud and rock, and woodland wet with
   spray!

III

O Goths and Vandals! Ye who'd weigh for
   gold
The rights of men, the joys of young and old!
Would ye enforce a claim to every sod
That fills the landscape? every bird that
   sings?
And every flower that lifts its face to God?
The Falls are rich in raiment of sweet grass,
And fern and moss and well-belovëd things
That droop not, neither pass,—
Heather and thyme and foxglove fair to see,
And broom and rowan-tree
That cling to earth as lichens to old walls!
And ye would ravish these, and stop the Falls
And make a desert of the forest free?

IV

Forbid it, Scotland! From the glens and moors,
From towns and cities, from the hills and plains,
Lift up your voice to spurn such sordid gains!
Say that your pride endures,—
Say that the seasons pass, but not your rights,
And not your portion in the days and nights,
And not the memory of your battle-shocks,
And not the vigils that your mountains keep
When moon and stars invest the purpling sky.
Say that the Falls are God's, who bade them leap
From those reverberate rocks,—
A dower divine which traders shall not buy!

SEA VOICES

I

DARKNESS and danger on the stormy deep !
The wandering waters, in their ceaseless
   sweep,
Half swamp the world, and wait no judgment
   day ;
And to the wild nor'easter that she loves
The ocean bares her breast,
And flings aloft great whiffs of sudden spray,
Like myriads of white doves ;
And, zenith-high, a jagg'd three-quarter moon
Drifts slowly towards her haven in the west,
Fainting for fear, lest dawn should come too
   soon.

II

How grand the scene? How weirdly through
    the night
The pallid orb leans outward from the clouds,
As if she heard the tempest in its flight,
Or saw the wreckages of years gone by,
Or ghosts in bursting shrouds
Come back with maniac-cry
To claim their share of plunder 'neath the sky!
Sees she the things that are?
The lifted hand of murder?—the torn sail
Of some crew-cursing ship that down the gale
Seeks jeopardy afar?
An idyl of sea-sorrow in a cave
Whose floors are sanded gold,—
Whose inmates are two lovers from a wreck?
Or knows she of adventures o'er the wave
With England's name for watch-word, as of
    old,

On some great quarter-deck
Whose aureole-flag is beauteous to behold?

III

With mighty pinions strong
The wet wind scuds along
To overtake the ships that bear home-news,
Ere yet the swift sea-mews
Have shrilled their boisterous matins to the
    storm,—
The while, with bulk enorme,
The snow-capped billows leap towards the
    sun,
Content when day's begun;
And, far and near, the winds and waves
    combine
To sing that chant divine
Which has for bass the thunder, and for lilt

The rain-drops that are spilt
Ere yet the rainbow-ridge has ceased to shine.

IV

Voices ascend for ever in all tones :—
Anger and joy and sorrow and deep awe,
And misery merged in moans
That have their place in nature's runic law,—
Voices that speak of menace and of mirth,
And thoughts unknown to earth ;
For who shall sift the secrets of the waves,
Or find the clue to countless sailors' graves,
Or bid the blustering Boreas cease to be ?
Our land's in league with all the winds that blow ;
And none shall count his gains, or friend or foe,
Till he's at one with us in his degree ;
And none can read the riddle of the years

Till he and his compeers
Have heard throughout our annals, loud and
  long,—
Like some imperial song,—
The wonders and the thunders of the sea.

THE QUELÉTZÛ

"Now the first bird that sang on earth was the Quelétzû."
—*Mexican Mythology.*

I

Up in the air,
Like a spirit in prayer,
With the wings of a dove, and the heart of a rose,
And a bosom as white as the Zàraby snows,
When the hurricane blows!

II

In the light of the day,
Like a soul on its way
To the gardens of God, it was loosed from the earth;

And the song that it sang was a pæan of mirth
For the raptures of birth.

III

The song that it sang
Like an echo out-rang
From the cloud to the copse, and the copse to the cloud;
And the hills and the valleys responded aloud,—
And the rivers were proud.

IV

If you think of the rush
Of the wind, and the flush
Of a morning of May when the sun is in view,

You will know what is meant by the flight
    from the dew
Of the first Quelétzû.

V

    If you think of these things
    You will dote on the wings
Of the wonderful bird in its upward career;
And the legends thereof will be sweeter to
    hear
Than the songs of a seer.

VI

    You will know what is meant
    By the pinioned ascent
Of an angel of grace when its mission is done,
And the knowledge of this will be second to
    none
Which the ages have spun.

VII

For the lark in its nest
Is a minstrel at best,
And the music it makes is the mirth of a kiss
That is flung to the skies in a frenzy of bliss
On the Morning's abyss.

VIII

And the nightingale's note
Is a sob from its throat,
And the gurgle thereof is a rapture of pain;
For the roses are sad,—and the lilies complain,—
When the silence is slain.

IX

All the larks in the world
With their feathers unfurled,

And the nightingales, too, in their tender
despair,—
All the birds that we know have a sorrow to
share
With the natives of air.

X

But the first Quelétzû
When it sprang to the blue,
Had the heart of a rose and the wings of a
dove;
And the song that it sang to the angels above
Was the music of Love!

THE DEAD TSAR

I

DEAD the great Tsar,—his hands upon his breast,
  His face unruffled 'mid a world's alarms,
And all his hopes and yearnings laid to rest,
  And all his prowess, all his latent harms;
  For nevermore, when trumpets call to arms,
Shall this man send his legions east or west.

II

He had the heart of one, the strength of ten;
  And with a patriot-zeal he sought to weld
Conflicting interests,—and to mend again
  The Code Imperial. For his fathers held

A strange dark place in history, which
　　impelled
To graver issues than were shown to men.

III

He probed the future; and, in his estate,
　　He saw the phantom of the Might-Have-
　　　　Been.
When he but spoke 'twas as the word of Fate;
　　And on his forehead was the lightning-
　　　　sheen
　　Of that great crown of his which few have
　　　　seen
Though all have guessed its glamour and its
　　weight.

IV

If ye would judge him rightly, say of him,
　　He lived and loved and suffered and was
　　　　brave!

A poisoner's hand had touched his goblet's
  brim,
A traitor's knife had marked him for the
  grave;
But he was one whom Fear could not
  deprave,
And Faith upheld him when his hopes grew
  dim.

V

The mountain sees the sun before the plain;
  But is it happier than the groves below?
  Are kings contented with a threatened reign?
    Do peaks of pride suffice them, and the
      snow
  Of upland winters,—when the vale's a-glow
With fruits and flowers, and fields of harvest
    grain?

VI

His very state oppressed him like a doom;
  His sceptre weighed him down; and, day and night,
He longed for that full freedom of the tomb
  Which all attain at last beyond the blight
  Of taunt and treason; and beyond the spite
That waits on Cæsars when their laurels bloom.

VII

A blameless life was his; and this will stand
  As his true record in the years to come.
He feared his God,—he loved his native land;
  He over-ruled intriguers in the sum
  Of all his vast designs; and he was dumb
When miscreants urged him to some fell command.

VIII

He would not loose his bloodhounds on the track
Of blue-eyed Peace,—his comrade when a boy.
He loved her ere he sought the strain and wrack
Of fierce and fond ambition, and the toy
Which men call Fame with all its base alloy
That some,—who know it well,—are proud to lack.

IX

We owe him much for what he left undone,—
For waste and want and noisome battle-deeds
Not wrought by him beneath his Russian sun.
For he had vowed to sow with better seeds

His fair domains, and foster grander needs
Than those foreshadowed ere his race was
    run.

X

A race of glory!—yet, beyond compare,
    A term of torture for a soul so just
That he could weep for others,—and could
    spare
    The wretch who wronged him by a broken
        trust,—
    And half forgive the felon's dagger-thrust
If one he loved besought him with a prayer.

XI

And Love was near him till his latest breath,
    And therewithal the comfort and the pride
Of that sweet hope which sprang from
    Nazareth;

And wan with tears, low-kneeling at his side,
The future Cæsar kissed a weeping bride
And took his charter from the lips of Death.

XII

Solemn the scene!—and tender and sublime
  That last leave-taking, when the requiem-
    bells
Rang out, on All Saints' Day, the dolorous
    chime
  That spoke of anguish mixed with fond
    farewells;
  And, far and near, in towns and citadels,
The tocsin tolling like the wail of Time!

A LOVE SONG

I

WHAT says the lark to the lea
When it leaps to the sun, and is free
With the freedom the poets acclaim
When they bow to the pomp of a name?
What say the eyes of the maid
To the lover whose lips are afraid?
It is Love that endureth for ever!

II

What says the breeze in its mirth
When it wakes to the wonders of earth?
What says the sea with its roar,
To the moon that is thrilled to the core,

A LOVE SONG

When the hurricane's having its way,
And the billows are bounding in spray?
It is Love that endureth for ever!

III

What says the poppy, unfurled,
To the sun that is king of the world?
What says the lily so white
To the rose that is red with delight,
When the lady I love is at hand,
And the summer is sweet in the land?
It is Love that endureth for ever!

THE DEATH-DAY OF TENNYSON

I

THE years have left their languors on his tomb,
  And day and night have watched him one by one
As two great Angels may, who know the doom
  Of all things made of flesh this side the sun;
  But he has gone where earthly pangs are done,
And no man knows the wherefore of the strife—
For Death has many names, and one is Life.

II

He could not perish! He but sank from sight,
As sinks the sun, effulgent in its sphere,
Which knows its heir-ship to the morning's light.
He died to live,—the Muse acclaims him here:
And he has gifts for all who hold him dear;
A song, an ode, a chant of quickening fire,
And matchless idyls lit with Love's desire.

III

There's not a bird can sing an April song
Without some apt remembrance of his verse,
Which one may hearken to a whole day long :—

A snatch of sorrow, sweet and sound and terse,
Or thrills of joy that haply will immerse
The eyes with tender tears in some lone vale—
For he was dowered as is the nightingale.

IV

He had his place in great Apollo's choir,
  And he could strike a note that was sublime
With all the witchery of a tuneful lyre,
  And all the cadence of a classic time.
  And he could put a sunset into rhyme,
And re-intone the lilting of the lark,
And fill the fields with music after dark!

V

He could unfold the riddle of the hours
  And tell us truths unknown to kings and queens,

And toy with grief, and play with passion-flowers,

And sing of Arthur's tilt-and-tourney scenes,

And hear the awful silence—what it means
When from the circuit of the cloudless skies
The lidless night looks down with all its eyes.

VI

He had a wand like Merlin,—'twas his pen,

And with a touch thereof he raised from earth

New domes of thought for women and for men,

And magic gardens made for love and mirth.

For all who knew him knew his poet-worth,
And how he caught the key-note of the spring
Because the birds had taught him how to sing.

VII

He loved our England, and in England's name
  He drew the sword of song, and flashed it
    high;
And with the trumpet of his Laureate fame
  He made it seem a goodly thing to die
    For God and Country,—with some battle-cry
That should be loud with love and fraught
    with fear
For men who doubt the truths they should
    revere.

VIII

He loved the rose, the lily of the field,
  The celandine, the wind-flower of the crag,
The daisy, fashioned like a little shield,
  The gorse that decks the pathway of the
    stag;

But most of all he loved the British flag,
And talked of it with tears of honest pride,—
We wrapt its folds around him when he died!

IX

He's safe with that,—as safe as heroes are
  Who front, for joy of some dear land's renown,
The flush, the frenzy, and the flame of war—
  Safe with the flag and with the laurel crown
  Of which no leaves have yet been trampled down;
Is there a man, in these degenerate days,
Worthy to win—and wear—such deathless bays?

THORNS

I

Come, little rose! and redly undeceive
  My soul to-day in mine extremity.
For I, of late, have learnt to disbelieve
The meekness of my maiden-paragon,
  Who hath, as one may see,
The fairest face the sun hath looked upon.

II

'Twas yester-week that, for an idle word,
  She did upbraid me, and, with sad surmise,
Did seem to doubt the truths I had averred.
I dared too much when I did make assaye

To front those fearless eyes;
And now I dwell apart, as night from day.

III

There's not much hope for me if she be filled
  With all this anger for her faithful friend.
The thoughts I crowned her with, are well-
    nigh killed
By her disdainful smile, and her distrust.
   Ah me! what tears I spend,
And what vain sighs, to urge her to be just!

IV

If she be kind to me 'tis always spring;
  If not, 'tis winter in the world of men.
Come, rose! and teach me how a tender thing
May move a maid to pity in my case,
   And I'll rejoice again
And wend my way to Love's abiding-place.

V

What! wilt thou wound me too, thou little rose!
And show a thorn, and use it unabashed
To call to mind anew the ways of foes
And woman's wrath a-kin to phantasy?
Or was't a whim that clashed
With something wild and unrestrained in
    thee?

VI

I like it not that roses so demure
    Should wear a weapon thus in ambuscade.
Whate'er my failings be my faith is pure;
And, moved thereby, methought a rose's flush
    Might stead me with the maid
Who is herself a rose of sweetest blush.

VII

But I'll not choose thee as my go-between
    To say how sad I am, and how distraught.

Of all the flowers of earth she is the queen
And would not laud thee for ungentleness.
   I know what grief has taught,
But what despair may mean I will not guess.

VIII

I'll keep thee here in token of an hour
   That comes not back,—a thing to ponder
      on
Within the sanctum of a starlit bower,—
A thing to wet with tears for love's delight
   When one's too woe-begone
To care for aught but anguish in the night.

IX

Be thou my heart's companion. See! I'll
   take
   Thy thorns from thee to press thee in the
      leaves

Of some quaint missal-book for sorrow's sake.
It will be sweet to know, when trees are bare,
   That Death,—which oft bereaves,—
Cannot despoil me of a flower so fair!

MOUSHKA

I

Who is my Moushka ? It is she
Who makes the world so fair to me;
  And with a glance,—a radiant one,—
Doth sanctify each sylvan nook;
Without the witchery of her look,
Without her love, I could not brook
  The gladness of the summer sun.

II

Though June has thirty nights and days,
I need them all to sing the praise
  Of her to whom my vows I bring,—
For she is pure as angels are

Who smile beyond the sunset-bar;
And from her name, as from a star,
   A wreathëd light is seen to spring.

III

If one should meet her in the glade
With all her golden hair displayed,
   And all a-flush, as now, with health,
He'd think the nymphs were come again,
And god Apollo, bold of reign,
Re-crowned for men on hill and plain
   With all the pomp of Doric wealth!

IV

He would not doubt that, Dian-wise,
She had descended from the skies
   To ratify the joys of May.
Her true-love eyes are full of dreams,
Her hair is lit with morning-beams

Whereof the world is proud, it seems;
And when she laughs, 'tis holiday.

V

She cannot hide her gentleness,
The happy smile, the looks that bless,
　The face that's like a flower to see,—
The lovely dimples in her arms,
The whispered words that act as charms,
To keep away all wanton harms
　When witches haunt the uplands free.

VI

And in her glances she reveals
A nature new to love-appeals,
　Which ne'ertheless is fond and meek.
She's naiad-like, and white as snows,
And hath the fragrance of the rose :—

And then I muse ;—The mirror knows,—
But who will make the mirror speak?

VII

To see her somewhere, all alone,
On rustic seat, as on a throne,
    And there to ache for very bliss,—
To sit beside her, face to face,
And breathe her breath a moment's space,
And then to die in her embrace,—
    Ah God! how glad a thing were this!

VIII

Who doubts of honour? Moushka's here;
And Moushka's eyes are brave and clear,
    And all her soul is sweet with love.
Her voice is like a silver bell,
And such delights about her dwell,

That fiends who frown in darkest Hell
Would smile to hear her spoken of.

IX

She hath few faults when all is told,
If she hath one; and young and old
Extol her grace and say of her,—
She's made of sunbeams and of flowers,
And dews and dawns and happy hours
And music breathed in Eden-bowers
When angels play the dulcimer.

X

If there be one I pity much,—
And there are myriads now of such,—
It is the man who has not seen
My Moushka's face, when, at a word,
Her maiden-blood, divinely stirred,

Makes blushing-time a hope deferred,
And me the suitor to a queen.

XI

She minds me of the life beyond ;
She sways me with a fairy's wand,
   And daunts me with her eyes of blue,
Till all my soul's to frenzy driven ;
For then,—be every sin forgiven !—
I know the nearest way to Heaven,
   But dare not urge a claim thereto.

XII

I dare not touch her where, apart,
She sits and smiles and breaks my heart,
   Or seems to break it all day long ;
A murmured word,—a frighted glance,—

A look that leaps to some romance
And yet is naught but fickle chance
   To do my soul a sudden wrong.

XIII

All this is true; I know it well.
But there's a secret left to tell
   Which I repeat for my delight,
In lonely hours unlooked upon,—
A secret sweet as songs of dawn
That linnets sing when mists are gone,
   And when the sun-god slays the night.

XIV

I were not wise would I not give
My claim to die, my power to live,
   And all my worldly hopes for this:

To know my loveliest Love is mine,
And that on me, with looks benign,
She hath conferred the right divine
　To crown her beauties with a kiss!

ODES

∴ *These Odes are now collected for the First Time*

THE ROYAL MARRIAGE ODE

SPECIALLY WRITTEN FOR THE NUPTIALS OF
THE DUKE AND DUCHESS OF YORK
ON JULY THE 6TH, 1893

I

WINTER has gone,—
The world is young again!
The jocund hours, careering in the train
Of this imperial day, will travel on
To hope and joy's fulfilment in the Land.
And hark! the cannon,—hark! the cannon's
  roar,
As loud as waves that lash the rocky strand,
When storm-delights are near,
And when the winds, exultant evermore,
Unfurl the glorious flag that we revere.

II

Ring out the joy-bells on the quickening air,
And let allegiance wait on ecstacy!
The world's in tune, to-day, with our desire,
And mirth and music make the morning fair,
And isle responds to isle, and sea to sea,
And all our thoughts aspire
To one majestic theme, and one acclaim,
In Love's transcendent name,
Which has for wreath a flame,
And is the rapt controller of the lyre.

III

It is a day of days,—
A day to boast of in futurity,
When Kings unborn, and nations yet to be,
Will read the record of the Land's renown,
And all the pomp and splendour of the Crown;

A day of days,—
A day to sing of, and to mark for praise,
In his great name for whom ancestral bays
Are bound with orange-flowers;
A day of days,—
A day in which are merged the linkëd powers
Of love and valour in the sunlit ways,
The lovely linkëd powers
Of grace and honour formed for unison,
And for the fulness of a Nation's pride:—
High-seated York and his elected Bride
Who wears, all through the year, the name of
    spring,
A May-Day name belov'd by queen and king
As earth herself is worshipped by the sun.

IV

Love! Love! Love!
The winds are wild with love

The winds and waves of all the seas are mad
With hope that maketh glad,
And fires the blood with frenzies undefined,
That flash from mind to mind,
And thrill the soul that else were dark and sad.

V

There's not a flower alive, and not a bird,
And not a woodland thing,
And not a wandering brook that is not stirred
By some solution of sweet euphony,—
As if the keynote of the golden spring
Were tossed from choirs above,
And tuned to concert-pitch to rhyme with love!
The fields a-shimmering vaguely all the morn,
Are proud to wave their poppies in the corn,
As if they, too, had banners and were free;

The lark, alert in heaven, is loud with song
And trills of summer in its tuneful prime,
And pairing-days in England's fair domain,
And trysting-hours gone by, that come again,
And love's delight that knows not any wrong:
So sweet it is to dream of sorrows slain!
The very breeze, mëandering o'er the thyme,
Doth seem to rhapsodise
On faith that lives, and hope that never dies,
As if the fields were richer for the ode
Of their true singer on his sunward road,
And soon would tempt him back from out the blue:
The cowslips huddle close, as gossips do
That talk of bridal hours and wedding-gear,
Whereof the thoughts entrance
The souls of men and maids all through the year.

The trees themselves are touched as with romance,
And every flow'ret has a look of cheer,
Whereof the birds take heed ;
And, like a moving army on the mead,
The miles of grass are all a-stir with life,
A million blades uplifted in the sun,
As if for joy of battles bravely won
In some delicious daintiness of strife!
And so, in towns and cities far and near,
The flowers of joy,—the posies passion-dear,—
Are worn as trophies, and, with little sighs,
Looked at by lovers who have guessed aright
The reasons of the redness of the rose,
And why the breeze is welcome when it blows
A word of wonder from that fairy shore
Where Love is blind no more,
But sees all things, and truly, with glad eyes!

VI

And now, as rings and swings, the wedding-chime,—
The chime we love to hear,—
The wind will bear the news, from clime to clime,
Of this great day, pre-ordered from Above
To consecrate the fame, from year to year,
Of England's sea that girds us round and round,—
The sun-surveying sea that, with its waves,
Invokes the Land we love,
And evermore, with more and more rebound
And mirth-commingled sound
Re-echoes, with its thunder-note sublime,
The teachings and the triumphs of the time.

VII

And lo! the Bride and Bridegroom where
    they come,
Their faces flushed with joy, and love-alit,
As, far and wide, the clarion and the drum,
With notes that inter-knit,
Announce the princely pageant, and the shout
Which proves that true allegiance is not dumb,
But Argus-eyed and voicëd like the sea,
When all its waves are out,
And when the wind,—that knows itself so
    free,—
Has put to sudden and contemptuous rout
The mists that late were gathered on the lea.

VIII

Oh, never yet was month, in all the girth
Of all the teeming earth,
A daintier one to note than this of ours;

And never yet were spring-begotten flowers
Of more entranced repute
Than these that speak in odours, all day long,
Of Love's enravishment,—
As though the lily's languor were a song
Out-breathëd from pure snows,—
As though the gamut of the quivering lute
Were intermixed with intermittent scent
And had the fragrance of the English rose.

IX

Ruler of Heaven, that with a lightning-flash
Dost eye the welkin, and, from star to star,
Dost count the myriads of mortality,
And art for ever, as Thine angels are,
Unseen of men this side the sunset-bar,
And hast Thy footfall on the tidal sea
In hours of calm, and when the tempests
    clash,—

Ruler supreme, unfailing in Thy might,
That hast, by day and night,
A Father's love, unfaltering to the end,
For all who skyward tend,
And evermore art prompt in Thy decrees,—
Look down on us, Thy people, and on these,
The children of the Children of the Throne,
For whom the bells intone
The loudest, proudest, most ecstatic notes
That e'er from molten throats
Have flung entrancement on the fields and
    bowers,
And towns and topmost towers,
Of this our Land of love and enterprise!
O Thou that hast Thy sanctum in the skies,
Beyond the spaces where the planets meet,
And watchest all Thy creatures from above
For countless æons that to Thee are hours,
Or minutes merely, or a pulse's beat

Betwixt the yea and nay of acted thought.

O Thou that in the fulness of fair love

Dost make from out the nothingness of nought

The surging millions of mortality,

And hast the thunder for Thine ancient voice,

And for Thy silence, death,—

And for the flux and influx of Thy breath

The rush and roll of ages that rejoice,—

Bless Thou, this day, the realm, as in the past;

Bless and defend our Kingdom of the Sea,

That all who turn to Thee

May find their solace here, from first to last,

And rout the foes of Freedom and of Right,

Who launch, in our despite,

The lie that's merged in mockery of all good.

Disperse them, Mighty God, with all their brood,

And make them fall,—as fall in hurricanes

The doomed, unbending trees,—

That, in the years to come, none such may sound
Their traitorous tocsin-bell on English ground,
Whereon, to-day, are heard the lilting strains
Of glory's interlude,
And Love's full chorus on the rapturous breeze!

X

Ring out, ring out, ye silver-sounding bells,
Ye praise-abounding bells,
That are intoned to-day
For thoughts that wake in May
The apt enthralment of remembered joys.
Ye seem to melt in prayer,—
Ye seem to soar on wings of tender poise
To rouse the realm from Sorrow's dark embrace,
And therewithal,—as fits a theme so fair,—
To bring the Past and Future face to face

In this our living Present by the grace
Of most High God !—Such joy about ye clings
Ye seem to tell of flowers and wedding-rings
New-sanctified by fervour of new praise
Of him to whom we raise
Our pæan-shouts of honour in Love's name :—
The Captain of the Comrades of the Flag,
A captain of such fame
As should be talked of on the loftiest crag
Of proud and prompt ambition, as of yore.
For there's no heart that's English to the core
But loves him well and beats for joy of him ;
And youthful eyes grow dim
As men rehearse the perils he has passed,
When, out upon the tearing, shuddering blast,
He has fulfilled new duties, not set down,
But done for pride of Country and of Crown !
For, his the look that all true sailors know,—
The look of blue-eyed seamen who, on shore,

Do talk of death and danger and the roar
Of rampant waves,—the wreckers of the foe!
The look of one at peace with all the world,
Who yet, full soon, with England's flag unfurled,
Would scale the heights of Duty!
His be the meed, and his the prize of beauty,
And evermore his name be named aloud
As one of whom the seas and lands are proud.

XI

Ring out, ring out, ye rapt, unerring chimes,
That with the lilt of rhymes
And with the madness of metallic mirth
Do seem to wake the earth
To new achievements of old prophecy;
Ring out, ring out, your triumph to the sky,
And tell again the truth-abiding tale
Of man and maid affianced in the sight

Of God Eternal whom the Fates obey!
Ring out from hill to dale,
From town to town, from street to furthest
  street,
That all who meet and greet
May hear the joy-bells in the wind's caress,
And Love's instalment in the roar of guns.
Aye! ring your changes all the livelong day,
Till day be merged in mellowness of night,
And night look down with orbs of blessedness
On these enravished, these new-wedded ones.

XII

It is the type of May in bright array
That with a prayer-full glance doth seem to say
"God keep the Kingdom safe!"—it is the
  May,
The gemmed, the joyous May that on us
  smiles,—

The Loved One of the Isles
Whose fame shall none dispute or disavow
As with her radiant, diamond-wreathëd brow
She bends from left to right,
And right to left with love-assenting eyes,
In this cortège of wonder and delight,
While shouts on shouts arise
To greet the spouse of England's future king.
For her approach is sweeter than the sight
Of hawthorn-buds that make the meadows
    bright,
And fringe the frondal garments of the year;
And, now July is here,
We know 'twas Heaven that brought us back
    the Spring
To magnify its sway;
And while the clamorous bells about us ring,
We dream of flowers that grow for us in
    May,—

The mignonette that loves a lonely spot,
The jasmine pale, the blue forget-me-not
That looks with little eyes all down the lanes
To watch for happy swains,—
And daisies, with the wimples they have on,
That drink the dews and drowsiness of dawn;
And that fair flower of youth,
The rose of York, the white rose of the hedge,
That was a warrior's pledge,
And is, to-day, a sailor's in all truth.

XIII

O month of May that hast the shape of one
Who loves the Land, and is the Land's
    delight,—
O May belov'd by all beneath the sun
Who love true-love to-day,—
The flower and dower of May,
Of our sweet English May!—

O month, proclaim'd in thy primeval might
As month of months for ever!—thou art her's,
And she is thine, thy sister, thy true friend,
In whom thy favours blend,
As dawn with day, as June with bright July,
With which the sun unceasingly confers,
To gild these pomps of ours that shall not die,
Though summer's self must surely come to end.
And since the nation claims her for its own
The sun looks down, approving, and elate,
From out the silence of his azure tent,
A king, far-seeing, on his golden throne
Who knows the lords of earth in their estate;
And this young Sailor Prince of high descent,
Acclaimed of all true men, by land and sea,
Where Freedom's fight, in England's name,
    is fought,—
The son of our good King that is to be,
Of whom 'tis said, and justly, that in thought,

In thought and word and deed, for life and death,
He loves the Land that quickened him with breath,
And, with the Land, this scion of his House
For whom the summer brings by its decree,
In this great day's carouse,
A wreath of beauteous and unceasing fame
That sanctifies and sweetens the good name
Of Her we bow to as God's Deputy!

XIV

O Maker of the margins of the deep,
On which are marked the tracings of the shocks
Of time and tide and tempest and old age,
In warm and wintry climes,
Where fears abide, and where the whirlwinds keep

Their ghostly revels in the caves and rocks,
And where the winds assuage
Their mid-day thirst at some fierce equinox.
O thou unwavering God, that many times
Hast joyed in Thy creation, and art just,
And boundless in Thy mercy, and Thy trust,
And art the splendid wearer of the robes
Of day and night, and on the rolling globes
Hast set Thy mark, and art Omnipotent,—
O thou dread Lord that with a breathëd word
Can'st make and unmake mountains and the meres
Of twice ten thousand years,
When the great depths are stirred,—
And hast the summers and the verdant springs
For Thine unfolding, and, when clouds are rent,
The whirl and swirl of winds that plough the waves,

Where poor Remembrance craves
The right to weep for wonder of dead things.
O Thou that makest morning out of night,
And darkness out of light,
And safety out of hopes untimely wreck'd,
And hast for smile the silence of the dawn,
And for Thy words the week-days that are
    seven,
Look down on these Thy children, Thine
    Elect,
Who wear the rose of rapture rained upon
By dews of dearest Heaven!

XV

Ring out, ring out, ye golden-voicëd bells,
Ye proudly-pealing bells,
And north and south, and east and west
    alwày,
As fits the fame of this fair marriage-day,

Make all your meanings clear, and therewithal
The trust that in us dwells,
That evermore, at love's and honour's call,
The Bride and Bridegroom of this hallowed time,
For whom we sound the chime,
May be a life-long lustre for us all.
Ring out, ring out, ye love-abiding bells,
Ye wildly-wakened bells,
Adown the moors, across the dales and hills,
Where blow the winds, where grow the daffodils,
And where the ways are strewn
With token-flowers bequeathed to us by June.
Oh, ring, ye bells, divinely as beseems
A day of sweetest dreams,
Which, by-and-by, the stars will sparkle to,
A-glittering through and through,

From out the welkin's warm and dizzy height;—
Ring out, ring out, and rend the air with notes
That meet and mix, and part and re-unite,—
As, with melodious throats,
Ye, hour by hour, proclaim
The rites of these, the Chosen of our Land,
Whom God, to-day, has joinëd hand in hand
For love, — for glory, — and for England's fame!

A CHORAL ODE TO LIBERTY

I

O sunlike Liberty, with eyes of flame,
    Mother and maid, immortal, man's delight!
Fairest and first art thou in name and fame,
    And none shall rob thee of thy vested right.
Where is the man, though fifty times a king,
Can turn the tide, or countermand the spring?
And where is he, though fifty times a knave,
Can track thy steps to cast thee in a grave?

II

Old as the sun art thou, and young as morn,
    And fresh as April when the breezes blow,
And girt with glory like the growing corn,

And undefiled like mountains made of snow.

Oh, thou'rt the summer of the souls of men,

And poor men's rights, approved by sword and pen,

Are made self-certain as the day at noon,

And fair to view as flowers that grow in June.

III

Look, where erect and tall, thy symbol waits,
  The gift of France to friends beyond the deep
A lofty presence at the ocean-gates
  With lips of peace and eyes that cannot weep;
A new-born Tellus, with uplifted arm,
To light the seas and keep the land from harm,—

To light the coast at downfall of the day
And dower with dawn the darkening water-
way.

IV

O sunlike Liberty, with eyes of flame,
  Mother and maid, immortal, stern of vow !
Fairest and first art thou in name and fame,
  And thou shalt wear the lightning on thy
    brow !

V

Who dares condemn thee with the puny
  breath
  Of one poor life, O thou untouched of
    Fate !
Who seeks to lure thee to a felon's death,
  And thou so splendid, and so love-elate ?
Who dares do this and live ? Who dares
  assail

Thy star-kissed forehead, pure and marble-
  pale ;
And thou so self-possessed 'mid all the stir,
And like to Pallas born of Mulcibèr?

VI

Oh, I've beheld the sun at setting-time
  Peep o'er the hills as if to say good-bye :
And I have hailed it with the sudden
    rhyme
  Of some new thought, full-freighted with a
    sigh.
And I have mused :—E'en thus may Freedom
    fall,
And darkness shroud it like a wintry pall,
And night o'erwhelm it, and the shades
    thereof
Engulf the glories born of perfect love.

VII

But there's no fall for thee; there is no tomb;
    And none shall stab thee, none shall stay
        thy hand.
Thy face is fair with love's eternal bloom
    And thou shalt have all things at thy
        command.
A grave for thee? Aye, when the sun is slain,
And lamps and fires make daylight on the
        plain,
Then may'st thou die, O Freedom! and for thee
A tomb be found where fears and dangers be.

VIII

O sunlike Liberty, with eyes of flame,
    Mother and maid, immortal, keen of sight!
Fairest and first art thou in name and fame,
    And thou shalt tread the tempest in the
        night!

IX

There shall be feasting and a sound of song
　In thy great cities; and a voice divine
Shall tell of freedom all the winter long,
　And fill the air with rapture as with wine.
The spring shall hear it, spring shall hear
　　　the sound;
And summer waft it o'er the flowerful ground;
And autumn pale shall shake her withered
　　　leaves
On festal morns and star-bespangled eves.

X

For thou'rt the smile of Heaven when earth
　　　is dim,—
　The face of God reflected in the sea,—
The land's acclaim uplifted by the hymn
　Of some glad lark triumphant on the lea.
Thou art all this and more! Thou art the goal

Of earth's elected ones from pole to pole,
The lute-string's voice, the world's primeval
    fire,
And each man's hope, and every man's desire.

XI

O pure and proud! O gentle and sublime!
    For thee and thine, O Freedom! O my
        Joy!
For thee, Celestial! on the shores of time
    A throne is built which no man shall destroy.
Thou shalt be seen for miles and miles around,
And wield a sceptre, though of none be
    crowned.
The waves shall know thee, and the winds of
    heaven
Shall sing thee songs with mixed and mighty
    steven.

XII

O sunlike Liberty, with eyes of flame
Mother and maid, immortal, unconfined!
Fairest and first art thou in name and fame,
And thou shalt speed more swiftly than the wind!

XIII

Who loves thee not is traitor to himself,
　Traitor is he to God and to the grave,
Poor as a miser with his load of pelf,
　And more unstable than a leeward wave.
Cursëd is he for aye, and his shall be
A name of shame from sea to furthest sea,
A name of scorn to all men under the sun
Whose upright souls have learnt to loathe this one.

XIV

A thousand times, O Freedom! have I turned
  To thy rapt face, and wished that, martyr-wise,
I might achieve some glory, such as burned
  Within the depths of Gordon's azure eyes.
Ah God! how sweet it were to guard thy life,
To aid thy cause, self-sinking in the strife,
Loving thee best, O Freedom! and in tears
Giving thee thanks for death-accepted years.

XV

For thou art fearful, though so grand of soul,
  Fearful and fearless, and the friend of men.
The haughtiest kings shall bow to thy control,
  And rich and poor shall take thy guidance then.

Who doubts the daylight when he sees afar
The fading lamp of some night-weary star,
Which, prophet-like, has heard amid the dark
The first faint prelude of the nested lark?

XVI

O sunlike Liberty, with eyes of flame,
  Mother and maid, immortal, prompt of
    thought!
Fairest and first art thou in name and fame,
  And thou shalt lash the storm till it be
    nought!

XVII

O thou desired of men! O thou supreme
  And true-toned spirit whom the bards
    revere!
At times thou com'st in likeness of a dream
  To urge rebellion with a face austere;

And, by that power thou hast,—e'en by that
    power
Which is the outcome of thy sovereign-dower,—
Thou teachest slaves, down-trodden, how to
    stand
Lords of themselves in each chivàlrous Land.

XVIII

The hosts of death, the squadrons of the law,
    The arm'd appeal to pageantry and hate,
Shall serve, a space, to keep thy name in
    awe,
    And then collapse, as old and out of date.
Yea, this shall be; for God has willed it so;
And none shall touch thy flag, to lay it low;
And none shall rend thy robe that is to
    thee
As dawn to day, as sunlight to the sea.

XIX

For love of thee, thou grand, thou gracious thing!
For love of thee all seas, and every shore,
And all domains whereof the poets sing
   Shall merge in Man's requirements evermore.
And there shall be, full soon, from north to south,
From east to west, by Wisdom's word of mouth,
One code of laws that all shall understand,
And all the world shall be one Fatherland.

XX

O sunlike Liberty, with eyes of flame
   Mother and maid, immortal, sweet of breath!
Fairest and first art thou in name and fame,
   And thou shalt pluck Redemption out of Death!

HYMN TO THE RISING SUN

I

Thou mighty Orb that on the Morning's brow
Dost shine, all-seeing, in the plenitude
Of thine up-rising through the Infinite !
Look down and bless the day that's now
    ordained,
And let the pæans of the pomp of earth
Be thine for ever, thou that art a king
    And hast the Orient for thy crowning-place
    And all the welkin for thy way of grace.

II

The sea is thine, the shores thereof are thine,
And all the haunts of men through all the
    zones ;

Yea, each created thing, all through the years,
All things are thine, to make thee paramount;
And there's no essence known, by sea or land,
That is not quickened by the sight of thee;
> No! there is nothing, earthward or in air,
> Which loves thee not with love beyond compare.

III

O holiest on the mountains! O thou sun
That art a portent and prodigy,
And evermore dost measure time and space!
To thee we turn, to see thee what thou art,—
How fair, how constant, and how girt with beams,
And how exultant in thy golden strength,
> When, one by one, the stars confess thy power
> And leave thee all the landscapes for a dower.

IV

Bless thou the hills, the rivers, and the plains,
The founts, the forests, and the foaming sea;
And each and all thy life-long suppliants!
Throughout the seasons of thy setting-time
Bless thou the winds which are thy mes-
    sengers;
And, in thy rising, bless thou every field
    And every harvest which thou shinest on,
    And every soul who claims thy benison.

V

O planet-prince! Thou glory born of night,
That, out of night, dost come to sway the
    world!
Behold, we love thee as the ancients loved,
When thou didst bear a god's name under
    Heaven.
For thou'rt the Regent of the King of Kings,

And His exponent through the centuries;
And all thy ways are wondrous, as of old,
When Sappho praised thee with her harp
of gold.

VI

A laureate-bird is thine in every grove;
In all the fields thou hast thy troubadours.
A thousand times the lark has trilled to thee,
And waked the woods in April and in May;
A myriad times, and more, his skyward notes
Have drenched the summer with the dews of
song,
And made, as 'twere, a feast-time overhead,
For bards to boast of when the days are
dead.

VII

Thou proud and prompt! Thou keeper of
the keys

Of East and West, which are thy heritage,
Where thou, — at soaring and at setting-
time,—
Dost hold a mansion, well-belov'd of men,
The roofs whereof are jasper and red light.
O jocund king! transcendent, unafraid,
　And unassailed by storms throughout the
land,
　Look down and bless the oceans thou hast
spanned.

VIII

Bless thou the workers and the men of
thought,
The work they do, the wonders of the lute,
And all the whisperings of the woods and
streams!
For thou'rt the wearer of the clouds of
morn,

And where thou art the hours are golden-
    wing'd,
And where thy servants are thy fame is great,
    And where thy singers are, in bower and
        town,
    The hearts of men respond to thy renown.

IX

Hear us, Light-Giver! and from dawn to
    dusk,
Be thou the fiery signal of much joy!
Unfurl thy banners beauteous on the hills,
And let the flash thereof,—thy blazonry,—
Be hope's fore-runner in the reddening meads.
O Sire of Seasons! Monarch of the Months!
    Illume us here, thy suppliants, on the sod,
    And lead us, through thy summers, up to
        God!

THE WHITE ROSE OF THE CROWN

Specially Written in Commemoration of the Birth of Prince Edward of York. June 23rd, 1894

I

Now has the golden year upon its way
Vouchsafed a blessing for the Land's delight;
And Grief, the bane of earth, has taken flight.
The year is thrilled with love, as on the day,
When York brought home the May,
And wedding-bells were clamorous all the morn
With messages to men.
For lo! to England's Crown a child is born,
A bud of hope, a rose without a thorn,
A little life whose emblem is a dove
New-sped from Heaven above
To be acclaimëd now by lute and pen.

II

The flag may well be proud to wave aloft
With all its tints unfurled,
The while the sun, effulgent, fair and soft
Looks down with fostering and benignant
    gaze
On him for whom are strewn, in gentle praise,
The token-flowers of joy from half a world.

III

Dear England's Child! be thine the nation's
    care,
The people's love throughout the years to
    come,
And earnest men thy servants in the sum
Of all their deeds for ever!
Glory be thine and danger track thee never;
And Misery, from the purlieus of its lair,
Make no complaints of thee in thine estate;

And Anarchy, whose dictum is of hate,
Collapse at sight of thee;
For Love is lord of all, in Childhood's name,
And knows not malice, or the touch of shame,
Or any lack of faith by land or sea.

IV

Now shall be heard the sky-saluting sound
Of patriot-voices, and the glad rebound
Of trump and cannon, famed in many fights,
That re-announce the rights
Of sceptred Freedom, our true heritage;
Nor shall we need a scroll or battle-gage
To prove its trustiness.
We have it safe; and with it,—ocean-wide
And clear as God has willed it,—the good news
Of leaguèd vows in lands that we possess
Out there, beyond the billowy, bounding tide

Where this great flag of ours absorbs the hues,
As earth and sky and sea, as all men know;
And how it scares the foe,
And how, to keep it pure and proud and high,
The best of us would kiss its folds,—and die!

V

But peace is with us, and the plenitude
Of power consorted with such equity
As fits the age we live in, and the free
And fearless Briton, born for precedence;
And with us, too, the hate of party-feud,
The cry for one vast union and the sense
Of England's mission, based on Brotherhood.
The world has learnt our lessons more than once,
And will again,—if one may read aright

The record of the guns,—
And therewithal the measure of the might
Of Albion's hero-sons,
Who, far and wide, have borne, and yet will bear,
Our lordly banner like a flame in air.

VI

Yet there's a sweeter thing than Fame's award,
Or mastery of the menace of the sword,
Or fear that brings the traitor to his knees,
Or meekness of a bride,
Or lilting of the lav'rock on the breeze
When dews of morn are dried.
There is a sweeter thing than all of these,
A purer thing than pardon, and a pride
Better than pomp or pageant in the land :—
It is the sinless hand,

The blameless touch of one such little child
As this whereon full tenderly have smiled
The Great Ones of the Realm!
And who shall say this offshoot of the Crown
Will not achieve renown
And gild anew the glories of his race
By God's abiding potency of grace
When foes would overwhelm?

VII

A dearer pledge than this can no man bring
To sanctify the sweetness of the spring,
Or give the radiant June a summer-sway
Of joy and splendour fit for holiday.
The weakness of a child is more than strength
Of mighty armies, when, at sceptre's length
From some Imperial Throne,
Which knows it for its own,
It smiles into the future all day long,

As if,—beyond our zone,—
It heard an angel's whisper through a song ;—
A babe is pure, a rose can do no wrong!

VIII

Let's talk to-day of England, and of times,
When men are moved, as by a spirit-call,
To do the deeds that ripen into rhymes ;
And when our banner, famous in all climes,
Asserts our ocean-prowess, and the thrall
Of Her whose rule is gracious to us all.
Let those be sad who must,—
Our hopes shall not be slain ;
Nor shall the sword of Empire go to rust!
All through the long and loved, triumphant
    reign
Of great Victoria, dear to English hearts,
This truth was ever plain,—
The Crown's the token of the Nation's trust,

And so shall prove, again and yet again !
The day comes, and departs;
The night annuls the sunset, and the sun
Rises to rule the morrow in God's name;
And,—like that Constant One,—
E'en like the spherëd blazonry of Heaven,
The circlet of the Sovereign brings us fame,
And blessings seven times seven ;
And who shall doubt the joys that we acclaim ?
The child we greet to-day will grow apace,
A boy, a man, a Briton true of soul,
Unmarred by stern control
Of adverse fate or evil wish fulfilled ;
And him the years will place
On such a height as Freedom's self hath willed !

ODE TO AN IDEAL POET

I

Singer of songs, immortal, unsurpassed,
That in the fulness of the flowering time
Of rapt, unerring rhyme
Hast made thyself a master among men,
And, with the witchery of a wayward pen,
Hast shown, from first to last,
The power thou hast to thrill us as with
    fire,—
Poet and seer and sounder of the lyre
That hast no rival underneath the sun
Since glorious Shelley comes not back
    again,—
Take thou the homage due to thy renown

As one for whom the seasons cannot frown.
Aye, take it, minstrel, for 'tis fairly won
By truth acclaimed, as at a Delphic shrine,
And that large love of freedom which is thine.

II

What need a crown for thee, what need a wreath,
And thou so sceptred in supremacy?
As leaps a sword from out its glittering sheath
So leaps the splendour of thy thought from thee.
In all the world there's none can sing as thou
Of grief and joy and glory in fair days,
And nights beyond all praise,
Wherein are heard, as in a languorous dream,
The throbbings of all lutes and dulcimers.
For thou hast been no breaker of the vow

That bound thee to the Brotherhood of Song.
Apollo met thee by his haunted stream
And there he filled thee with the fire that stirs
Thy soul to-day, to make thee passion-strong.
No bard is like to thee in all the Land
Which knows thee, and is glad of thee, and proud,
And names thy name aloud
As first and foremost of the singing-band.

III

If there be greater bards let them appear!
If there be one alive to cope with thee
Let's hear his song! If he can strike the chords
As thou, from year to year,
Let's own his skill in such high minstrelsy!
All praise to him who takes divine awards

Beyond thy teaching, if such man there be.
But there's none such in this world's way-
    wardness;
And like a pæan is the proud caress
Of thy sweet singing of the sea-ward joys;
For thou'rt an ocean-lover; and as brave
As Byron was to wanton with the wave;
And, in the Maytime of the verdant plains,
When we are sheltered from the winter's ban
And spring and winter hold the world in poise,
Thou dost renew the rapture of the strains
That tell of freedom and the hopes of Man,
And doubts dissolved, and dangers that are
    gains,
And lapse of battle-pains;
And love and laughter born of little sighs,
And comfort of the kissing of closed eyes!
And one may guess, in brooding on thy
    words,

That all the woodland ways are known to thee,
And all the secrets of the singing-birds,
And all the mirth and madness of the sea.

IV

Thou hast a song for every day's desire,
And every hour's enthralment and behoof;
And, from the thunder-cloud of thy reproof,
The lightning of thine anger flashes forth;
A tongue of searching and persistent fire,
To reprimand the despot in his might
And plead for those who combat for the Right!
For none can still the sea, or quell the wind,
From east to west, from south into the north,
Or build anew the rainbow when 'tis torn;
And none can curb the clamours of the mind,
Or kill a thought new-born.

V

Oh, thou'rt as free as storms at equinox;
And with thy lyrics, as with battle-shocks,
Thou dost assail the foes of humankind
Who cringe on supple knee,—
Let such beware of thee!
For, should the best of them betray their trust,
Thy trenchant word would bring them to the
    dust.

VI

But hate absorbs thee not; thy theme is love,
And all the joys and all the griefs thereof
Which all the years unfold.
Thy hand is strong; thy lute-strings are of
    gold;
And thou, as Chaucer did in days gone by,
Can'st wake the world to wonder and delight,
And through the courts and corridors of fame

Can'st make thy voice ring out, by day and
    night,
In full-toned ecstacies of earth and sky.
Thou hast for badge a star, for faith a flame,
And for thy meed the halo of a name;
Thy peers are with the dead who cannot die!

THE SONG OF THE FLAG

I

Up with the flag!
And let the winds caress it fold on fold,—
For 'tis the token of a truth sublime,
A flag of pride, a splendour to behold!
And 'tis our honour's pledge:
A thing to die for, and to wonder at,
When, on the shuddering edge
Of some great storm, it waves its woven joy
Which no man shall destroy,
In shine or shower, in peace or battle-time.
Up with the flag!
The winds are wild to toss it, and to brag
Of England's high renown,—
And of the throne where Chivalry has sat

Acclaimed in bower and town
For England's high renown,—
And of these happy isles where men are free
And masters of the sea,
The million-mouthëd sea,
That calls to us from shore to furthest shore,—
That fought for us of yore,—
The thunder-throated, foam-frequented sea
That sounds the psalm of Victory evermore!

II

For England's sake, to-day,
And for this flag of ours which, to the blast,
Unfurls in proud array
Its glittering width of splendour unsurpass'd,—
For England's sake,
For our dear Sovereign's sake,—
We cry all shame on traitors, high and low,
Whose word let no man take

Whose love let no man seek throughout the
  Land,—
Traitors who strive with most degenerate
  hand
To bring about our Country's overthrow.

III

The sun reels up the sky, the mists are gone,
And overhead the lilting bird of dawn
Has spread, adoring-wise, as for a prayer,
Those wondrous wings of his,
Which never yet were symbols of despair.
It is the feathery foeman of the night
Who shakes a-down the air
Song-scented trills and sunlit ecstacies.
Aye, 'tis the lark, the chorister in gray,
Who sings hosannahs to the lord of light,
And will not stint the measure of his lay,
As hour to hour, and joy to joy succeeds.

For he's the morning-mirth of English meads;
And we, who mark the moving of his wings,
We know how sweet the soil whereof he sings,—
How glad the grass, how green the summer's thrall,
How like a gracious garden the dear Land
That loves the ocean and the tossed-up sand
Whereof the wind has made a coronal;
And how in spring and summer, at sunrise,
The birds fling out their raptures to the skies,
And have the grace of God upon them all.

IV

Up with the flag!
Up, up betimes, and proudly speak of it;
A lordly thing to see on tower and crag
O'er which,—as eagles flit
With eyes a-fire, and wings of phantasy,—

Our memories hang superb !
The foes we frown upon shall feel the curb
Of our full sway; and they shall shamèd be
Who wrong, with sword or pen,
The Code that keeps us free.
For there's no sight, in summer or in spring,
Like our great standard-pole,
When round about it ring
The cheers of Britons, bounden, heart and soul,
To deeds of duty dear to Englishmen ;
And he who serves it has a name to see
On Victory's muster-roll ;
And he who loves it not, how vile is he !
For 'tis the wave's delight,—
Our ocean-wonder, blue and red and white ;
Blue as the skies, and red as roses are,
And white as foam that flashed at Trafalgàr ;
The wind's and wave's delight,

The badge and test of right,
Girt with its glory like a guiding-star!

V

The wind has roared in English many a time,
And foes have heard it on the frothy main,
In doom and danger, and in battle-pain;
And yet again may hear
In many a seaward, sun-enamoured clime.
And how the hearts of traitors ache with fear
When our great ships go forth, as heretofore,
Full-armëd from the shore,—
And Boreas bounds exultant on the seas,
To bid the waves of these,—
The subject-waves of England and the Isles,—
Out-leap for miles and miles,
As loud as lions loosed on enemies!

VI

Oh, may no mean surrender of the rights
Of our ancestral swords,
Which made our fathers pioneers and lords,
And victors in the fight,—
May no succession of the days and nights
Find us or ours at fault,
Or careless of our fame, our island-fame,
Our sea-begotten fame,—
And no true Briton halt
In his allegiance to the Victory-name
Which is the name we bow to, in our thought,
When English deeds are wrought
In lands that love the languors of the sun,
And where the stars have sway,
And where the moon is marvelled at for
    hours.
The flags of nations are the ocean-flowers,
And our's the dearest, our's the brightest one,

That ever shimmered on the watery way
Which patriots call to mind,
When they remember isles beyond the dawn
Where our sea-children dwell.
For there's no flag afloat upon the wind
Can wave so high, or show so fair a front,
Or gleam so proudly in the battle-brunt,
Or tell a tale of conquest half so well
As this we doat upon!

VII

The storm is our ally, the raging sea
Is our adherent, and, to make us free,
A thousand times the full-tongued hurricane
Has bellowed forth its menace o'er the deep;
And when dissensions sleep,
When sleep the wrought-up rancours of the
    age,
We shall again inscribe, and yet again,

On History's glowing page
The story of the flag,—
For 'twas our Nelson's flag
Which none in all the world shall put to shame,
Or vilify, or blame,—
The story of the glory of the flag
Which waved at Waterloo,
And was from first to last the symbol true
Of Wellington's pure fame.

VIII

High, high the flag for England's sake and our's,
Who know its vested powers
And what it means, in wartime, and in peace
When fierce contentions cease,—
High, high the flag of England over all,
Which naught but good befall!

High let it wave, in triumph, as a sign
Of Freedom's right divine,—
Its glorious folds out-fluttering in the gale,
Again to tell the tale
Of deeds heroic, done at Duty's call!
The wind's our trumpeter; and east and west,
And north and south, all day,—as on a quest,—
It bears the news about
Of all we do and dare, in our degree,
And all the Land's great shout,
And all the pomp and pageant of the Sea!

www.ingramcontent.com/pod-product-compliance
Lightning Source LLC
Chambersburg PA
CBHW030301170426
43202CB00009B/834